For my great-nieces and great-nephews: Millie, Henry, Rory, Declan, Harper, Levi, Sam, Noah, Easton, and Shea. Follow your own light. —K.K.

For Grampy, the world's greatest chocolate chip cookie connoisseur —L.B.S.

To my grandpa —R.K.

Text copyright © 2023 by Lowey Bundy Sichol and Kathleen King
Jacket art and interior illustrations copyright © 2023 by Ramona Kaulitzki
All rights reserved. Published in the United States by Random House Children's Books,
a division of Penguin Random House LLC, New York.

Random House and the colophon are registered trademarks of Penguin Random House LLC.

TATE'S® and TATE'S BAKE SHOP® are trademarks owned by Mondelez Inc., used with consent.

Visit us on the Web! rhcbooks.com

Educators and librarians, for a variety of teaching tools, visit us at RHTeachersLibrarians.com

Library of Congress Cataloging-in-Publication Data is available upon request.
ISBN 978-0-593-48566-8 (trade) — ISBN 978-0-593-48567-5 (lib. bdg.) — ISBN 978-0-593-48568-2 (ebook)

The artist used Adobe Photoshop to create the illustrations for this book.
The text of this book is set in 16-point Clearface MT Std.
Interior design by Elizabeth Tardiff

MANUFACTURED IN CHINA
10 9 8 7 6 5 4 3 2 1
First Edition

COOKIE QUEEN

HOW ONE GIRL STARTED TATE'S BAKE SHOP®

BY **KATHLEEN KING** AND **LOWEY BUNDY SICHOL**

ILLUSTRATED BY **RAMONA KAULITZKI**

Random House 🏠 New York

It was very early in the morning when Kathleen stepped into the kitchen.

Kathleen was only eleven, but each morning she made her own breakfast and packed her own lunch for school—and when her parents worked late, she whipped up dinner for her brothers and sister.

Kathleen enjoyed cooking, but more than anything, she loved to bake.

On this particular morning, Kathleen mixed the ingredients . . .

. . . and then she scraped the sticky dough into little mounds.

Then she dropped them onto the baking tray . . .

. . . and then she put them into the oven for nine minutes exactly.

Hmmm . . . They were good, but too puffy and too gooey. Kathleen liked her cookies thin and crispy. But these would have to do for now.

Kathleen placed the warm cookies onto a platter and carried them

past the chickens scratching for their morning meal . . .

past the cats chasing after a field mouse . . .

past the cows heading into the pasture . . .

. . . down to her family's farm stand.

Her father, Tate, was already there, filling wooden shelves with ripe raspberries, juicy blueberries, and crisp beans from their garden.

Last night, Kathleen and her father had made a deal: If Kathleen baked cookies and sold them at the farm stand every day that summer, she could keep *all the money* she earned to buy new clothes for school.

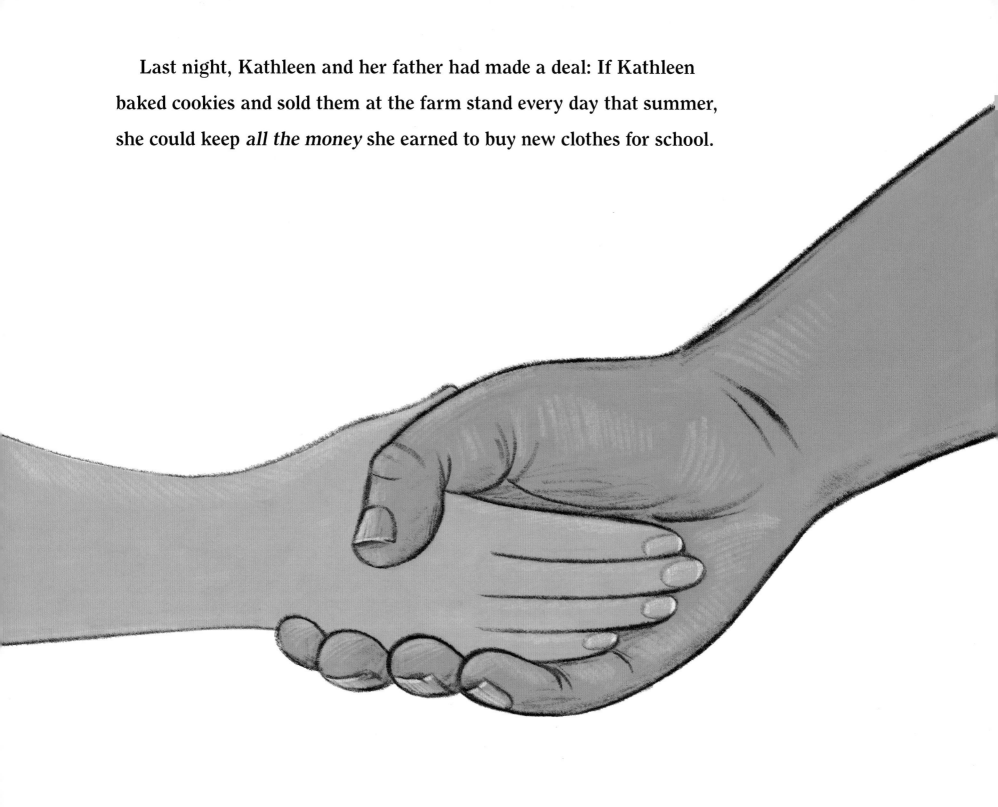

"How are Kathleen's cookies today?" her father asked.

"Good, I guess." Kathleen sighed. "But not quite right.
I believe I can make the best cookie ever."

Early the next morning, while the piglets slept soundly in the barn, Kathleen stepped into the kitchen.

She started to experiment: A little more baking soda. A little less salt. A lot more sugar.

Not quite right.

Then: A little more flour. A lot more salt. A little less sugar.

Still not right. So she tried again. . . .

A little less flour.

And again. . . .

More chocolate chips.

And again. . . .

One more egg.

And again. . . .

Two fewer eggs.

And again and again and again. Kathleen's cookies were always good,
but they were not thin and crispy—and they were not the best cookie ever.

Then one day . . .

"What haven't I tried?"

More butter. More *salted* butter!

"How are Kathleen's cookies today?" Tate asked.

"Great: just the way I like them. But how do I make them so they're the *only* cookies people want to buy?"

"There's one way to find out . . . ," Tate suggested.

At every farm stand, the same chocolate chip cookie was for sale.

Just as she suspected . . . small and puffy. Or soft and gooey.

"What do you think, Kathleen?" Tate asked.

"Not as good as mine, and they're all so small. I wish they were really, really . . . BIG!"

Early the next morning, before their rooster woke the farm, Kathleen stepped into the kitchen. She measured and mixed and added more butter. More *salted* butter, just like last time.

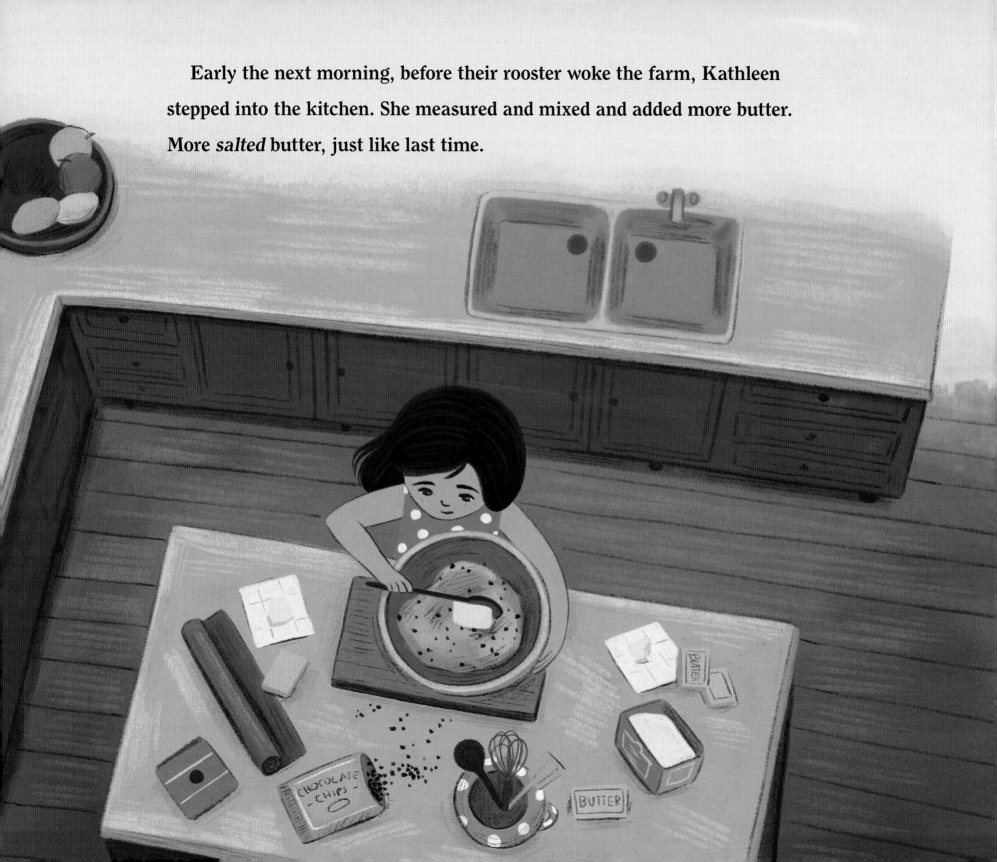

But this time, she also pulled out a big wooden spoon.

She dipped it into the sticky dough with a confident smile.

"How are Kathleen's cookies *today*?" Tate asked.

"Daddy, I did it! These are the best cookies ever."

They were thin and crispy—just the way Kathleen had always wanted them to be. And now each cookie was the size of a small plate.

But how should she sell them? Fortunately, Tate knew just what to do next.

"You have to give customers a deal they can't resist," he explained.

Tate helped Kathleen place six cookies into plastic bags and tie them with pretty ribbons.

Then they hung up a sign announcing the arrival of Kathleen's Cookies.

Word spread quickly. People came from small towns and big cities to visit North Sea Farms for fresh eggs and sweet fruit—but mostly for Kathleen's enormous, buttery-rich chocolate chip cookies.

Kathleen had found something she loved doing, something she hoped to do for a very long time. Whenever she closed her eyes, she could see it perfectly—Kathleen King: Cookie Queen—and it felt like the very best dream come true.

This is the true story of Kathleen King and how she started her cookie business at age eleven. Kathleen baked cookies for the family farm stand every summer for nine years. And every summer, customers came from far and near for her famous chocolate chip cookies. Kathleen earned so much money baking cookies that she was able to buy herself new clothes for school every fall and a car when she turned sixteen! When Kathleen was twenty, she opened her first bakery and named it Kathleen's Bake Shop. Twenty years later, she started a cookie company called TATE'S BAKE SHOP®, which she named after her loving father. Today, TATE'S BAKE SHOP® cookies are sold in grocery stores all over the United States, and the chocolate chip cookies have won many Best Chocolate Chip Cookie awards! Kathleen's story proves that kids can start great companies.

Kathleen's Cookie Recipe!

Kathleen & Tate's Molasses Cookies

This is the first cookie Kathleen baked with her father.

2½ cups (11½ ounces) all-purpose flour

½ teaspoon baking soda

¼ teaspoon salt

1 teaspoon ground ginger

½ teaspoon ground cinnamon

¼ teaspoon ground cloves

½ cup (4 ounces) salted butter

1 cup (7 ounces) granulated sugar

1 egg

1 teaspoon vanilla

½ cup milk

½ cup molasses

Preheat oven to 350 degrees. Line two sheet pans with parchment paper.

In a medium bowl, combine flour, baking soda, salt, ginger, cinnamon, and cloves.

In a large bowl, cream butter and sugar. Add the egg and vanilla, then the milk and molasses. Mix and scrape bowl.

Add the dry ingredients, and mix until combined.

Using two teaspoons or a two-tablespoon ice cream scoop, drop cookie dough onto sheet pans.

Bake 10–12 minutes, until center springs back when touched.

Cool on wire cooling rack, or leave on trays. Enjoy!

Yield: 32 cookies

Notes: If you like a spicier cookie, double the spices. Cookies can also be iced on top with your favorite cookie icing or glaze. Orange zest can be added to the glaze.

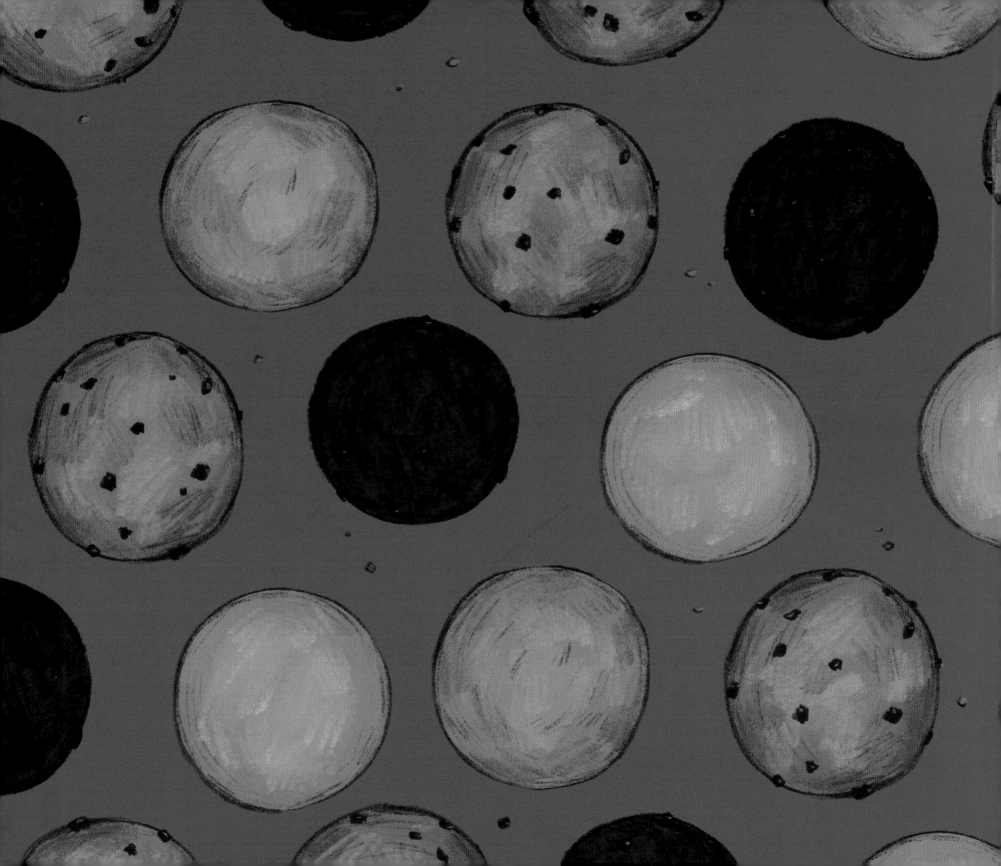